Cats from the Scandinavian Woods

A Study of Norwegian Forest Cats

Produced by Just Print IT! Publications
59 The Whaddons, Huntingdon, Cambs., PE18 7NW
Tel: 01480 450880

ISBN 1 902869 05 2

First Edition

CATS FROM THE SCANDINAVIAN WOODS

FOREWORD

Over the past two decades, Norwegian Forest Cats have found their way into so many homes and hearts, yet still there is no book written about them in the English language. Newcomers to the breed inevitably ask, "What books can I read?" and it is difficult to recommend any titles to date. All-breed cat manuals, encyclopædias and specialist magazines offer very little information on the "Wegie", and what material and pictures they do provide is often incorrect. This short study seeks to remedy this sad state of affairs. The author lives with nine fine Forest Cats of varying ages, and has eagerly sought out material and background information from general reference books, history books, folk tale collections, fellow breeders at home and abroad and last but not least, by "surfing the World Wide Web". She is still learning, so would welcome additions and corrections from those more knowledgeable than she is. All feedback is most appreciated!

Mary-Rose Douglas, Summer 1999

Introduction

All cats have secrets, and maybe Norwegian Forest Cats possess more than most. Although their origins are swathed in the mists of centuries past, it is clear that this is a very natural breed, and unlike many pedigree cats the appearance and character of the Norwegian Forest Cat has been fashioned by nature, not by man. They are known in their native land as the "faerie cat" (huldrekatt) because of their mysterious flitting amongst the trees, fast-moving and elegant in spite of their large size. It is not surprising to learn that these resourceful animals have long been the companions of isolated Norwegian farmers, in a mutually beneficial relationship. When Norwegians go out in their native wilderness they can still sometimes catch a glimpse of a wild Forest Cat, although most of them have sensibly settled amongst the homesteads and fishing villages which enable them to thrive. Nowadays they can increasingly be found in the apartments of Oslo and Stockholm, as modern Scandinavians treasure their native cat and enthusiastically play a part in the breed's preservation. The adaptability of the Norwegian Forest Cat means that they can comfortably settle into an indoor way of life so long as there's plenty of food and company.

Although Norwegian Forest Cats are to a large extent wild, and certainly blend effortlessly into the rugged landscape of Norway, their long association with mankind means that they are also quite prepared to be friendly. In fact, those that live as family pets are exceptionally affectionate and responsive. They have been welcomed by the natives of Scandinavia for much longer than the native British moggy has been tolerated in the UK, where cats were mercilessly persecuted as recently as the seventeenth century. Maybe this long association with mankind is why Norwegian Forest Cats are so fond of human company.

"Viking Kitten"
©R Jonker (Möre og Romsdal)

PHYSIQUE

It is easy to see how Norwegian Forest Cats are well equipped for survival in one of the harshest climates in the world. Their most important physical characteristic is the special waterproof top coat, covering a thick insulating undercoat, so that even when rain and sleet strike they remain cosy and dry next to the skin. This coat is nothing like the soft, fluffy coat of the Persian, which gets dangerously knotted if left unattended for any length of time. The coat of the Norwegian Forest Cat is largely self-maintaining, and they are also less prone to fur-balls than many breeds. Under the smooth top-coat is an insulating woolly undercoat, which consists of many soft hairs which grow so close together that they trap warm air in between, so that the cat has in effect its own portable duvet! Protecting these soft, slightly crinkled undercoat hairs are long, strong, straight guard hairs which are much coarser than the undercoat hairs and are covered in a thin layer of oil, so as to be weatherproof. The guard hairs form a shiny coat over the cat's back and down its sides, while the underside of the cat has no guard hairs, although the dense undercoat on the cat's tummy and lower chest

©A&P Bowler (Skjonn)
Female in summer coat still showing good ear tufts, furnishings and toe tufts.

contain protective oils too.

The official term for a Norwegian Forest Cats' coat is "semi long haired". This refers not only to the fact that the cats have much longer coats in winter than in summer, but also that the hairs are not as long as a true longhair (Persian) which will have been bred specially to have an extremely full, soft coat. Norwegian Forest Cats can develop impressive ruffs in cold weather, but their coats should never be fluffy or dry (lacking in oil). The shape of the coat is also important, and again quite different from that of a Persian. The ruff, or frill, should contrast with shorter hairs across the shoulder blades, and the breeches which become bushy in winter end in shorter fur over the lowest joint of the back leg. Rudimentary shaping of the coat can often be seen in even very young kittens. A cat with even-length fur all over is incorrectly coated - even if the fur is luxuriant. There should be a clear distinction in both length and quality of top coat and undercoat. A full mane, shirtfront and knickerbockers are developed for winter and then rapidly moulted again in late spring - so that by midsummer the big-coated cat has become comparatively sleek. The longer guard-hairs lie flat against the body in warm conditions so that only the plumed, bushy tail reminds us that this is, after all, a semi-longhaired cat. Of course, the lower the temperature and more prolonged the winter, the thicker and longer the coat will grow.

Large-boned and well-covered, Norwegian Forest Cats' solidly muscled bodies and thick legs have proportionately big paws which have special tufts of hair growing between the toes, actually covering most of their pads like a warm pair of snow-shoes. These large paws will also help the cat not to sink into the snow, which lies on the ground for many months in their native land. Their long, thick tails are another useful weapon against icy temperatures, as they not only help to balance the cat when active but can be wrapped protectively around the nose when sleeping. The claws are extra long and curved, extremely useful for climbing rock-faces which would be insurmountable to other cats. Even as kittens these huge talons are in evidence, but fortunately the Norwegian Forest Cat is gentle and intelligent, so scratches are rare. Their claws can also be used for hooking fish out of ponds and streams, for in their natural environment Wegies are adept at catching fish, being unafraid of water. Equally at home in a modern domestic setting, they will often "fish" a bar of soap out of their human's bath instead!

©R Jonker

Fine example of a full-grown blue classic tabby male in his prime. This cat has achieved Best in Show on many occasions.

The Wegie's long legs carry them high enough to avoid too much snow clinging to their long tummy fur, while the hind legs are longer than the back to enable athletic feats of running, jumping and above all, climbing. Unusually, Norwegian Forest Cats will usually descend a tree head first, in an efficient and confident spiralling motion.

Above all, perhaps the thing you first notice about a Norwegian Forest Cat is its noble head, which is a triangular shape with long straight nose and special expression of wild grandeur. The chin should be firm while the muzzle is almost pointed, not blunt and boxy. From the side, the line from nose tip to bottom of chin should be vertical rather than receding, while the chin itself should have depth. The eyes are not round and bold, but although well-opened and alert looking, they should have a slightly oblique set which results in an almond shape. Any sweetness of expression is incorrect once the cat is an adult. (Obviously it is very difficult for kittens *not* to look sweet, but even so, it is surprising at how early in its life a good Wegie kitten can get that typical Norwegian Forest Cat expression!) Their ears, though quite large, are well furnished with long hair to protect them, and they should have striking lynx-like tufts at the top although many cats are unfortunately seen without this "finishing touch". These ears are set high and open with good width at their base, so that the outer edge of the ears forms a line that is followed down the side of the cat's triangular "face". The size and position of the ears means that there is not a lot of space between them - often described as distance between the ears being less than the width of the base of one ear. The ears should also be pointed in shape rather than rounded, which adds to their appearance as that of an alert, finely-tuned hunter.

Thus it is a combination of head shape, ear set, expression in the eyes and carriage that bestows the unique Norwegian Forest "look". The males are particularly large, often growing to well over a stone or even a stone and a half in weight, while full-grown females are considerably smaller at 9 to 12 pounds on average. Size helps them to keep warm in their cold native climate, and I often find my Forest Cats seeking out draughts near doors and windows in my centrally-heated house. They really do seem to have a different metabolism from other breeds, and more than one owner has reported that outdoors her stud cat positively emits heat to the touch, even in the coldest weather, rather like a living radiator! Given the chance, a Norwegian Forest Cat will often curl up for a snooze in a frozen garden, so that the outside of his coat becomes encrusted with frost. Sinking your fingers into the coat you will soon feel that the cat is much warmer than you are!

Wegies are slow-maturing cats, and will take three or four years to fully develop. Different breeding lines develop at different rates. Younger cats should still have good boning and an elongated structure, but their frames will remain rangy for the first two or even three years of their lives, until their generous bone-structure is filled out with solid muscle by the time they reach their prime. The tail should be the same length as the body, so that a full-grown male will often measure more than one metre from nose to tail tip. The coat of a Forest Cat also takes some time to mature, and it is usually much better in both quality and quantity during its second winter than during its first.

©R Jonker
This brown tabby and white Forest Cat has a shorter head but excellent coat quality.

For centuries these rugged cats have thrived in the cruel, beautiful surroundings of Scandinavia, where temperatures of minus 40°C are not unknown. During the short, warm summer of their native land they shed their woolly undercoats and take the chance to breed sturdy kittens before the chill of autumn sets in. Even when they live in a centrally-heated environment, or a warmer country, they still follow the seasons with their coats - though to a lesser extent. Although the Forest Cat loses a lot of fur in a short time during March or April, the moult is no more troublesome than that of many short-coated breeds. The woolly undercoat comes out in cotton-wool-like balls, easily picked off clothes and carpets, and then there is very little shedding for the rest of the year. Conversely, many short-haired cats moult a little all year round, and their short but stiff, pointed fur weaves its way into fabric in a way that is very difficult to clear up!

©M Lindstedt (Frostnattens)
This young brown tabby, photographed in Sweden, has not yet developed her winter coat, though she has super type. Brown tabbies often take longer to grow their coats, which are nonetheless of good waterproof texture.

HISTORY

Where did these magnificent creatures originally come from? As there are no small cats indigenous to Scandinavia, they must have originally come from further afield. Maybe this map gives us a clue. A hoard of gold was deposited at Hon, south west of Oslo, in the second half of the ninth century, containing Arabic, Byzantine, English and Frankish coins, together with large neck-rings from Russia, which illustrates just how widely travelled the Vikings were.

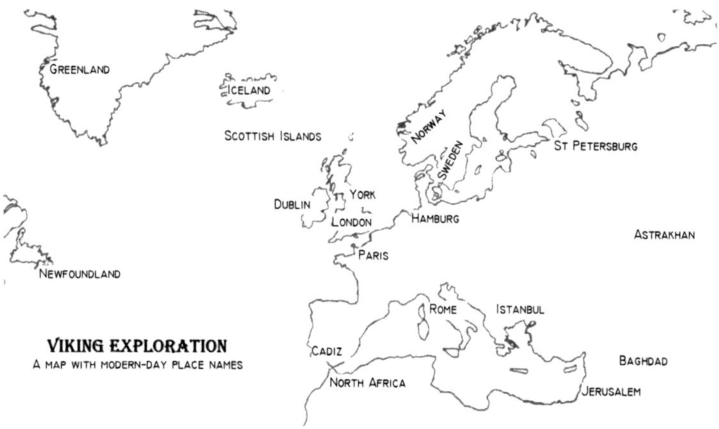

VIKING EXPLORATION
A MAP WITH MODERN-DAY PLACE NAMES

In fact the Viking world stretched from Newfoundland in the West to Reykjavik and Trondheim in the North, spreading as far as the River Volga in the East and right down to Baghdad, Jerusalem and North Africa in the South. Now we all know that ships need cats in order to control the rodent population (Captain Cook once had so many rats on board that he had to make a special call at a south-sea island in order to disgorge his unwelcome guests. The rats scurried ashore and decimated the local wildlife.) So it is almost certain that these doughty Viking sailors took on board cats encountered all over their world. In fact, many of the colours found in Norwegian Forest Cat populations relate to colours common in Turkey but rare across the rest of Europe, another pointer to the Vikings having brought cats across their trade routes from the Byzantine East. It is worth noting here that several Byzantine emperors had Scandinavian guards, known as the Jaeringer, so there was a lot of commerce between the two nations. In particular, the "Snow Cats" (pure white Forest Cats) are reminiscent of the elegant silky-white Angoras from Turkey.

There would also have been Russian Blue-type animals with their plush grey coats; ticked ancestors of today's Abyssinians from North Africa; and, of course, ordinary European Moggies in shades of silvery brown tabby or black and white. Spain probably contributed the tortoiseshell variation (the Vikings spent some time in Cadiz and Córdoba – nowhere with a navigable river was safe from

©A Robinson (V Hoar/Galadrial) Grand Champion Female

their adventuring).

It has sometimes been suggested that Forest Cats may have partly originated from Scottish Wild Cats too, but I think this unlikely as the Scottish cats are impossible to handle right up to the present day, even when hand-reared from birth. I'm sure that the Vikings would have chosen cats with as trouble-free a character as possible to join them on their travels. Whatever their place of birth, when these cats were brought home to Scandinavia they would have had a harsh environment to contend with, so would gradually have evolved into the large-boned, heavy-coated, many-coloured animals which we know and love today. We'll have to make sure that, with the luxuries of warmth and readily available food now afforded to them, we never forget that they should remain truly rugged!

Freya's Chariot
Reproduced courtesy of Frances Matthews (Dovregubben)

As early as the 16th century, Norwegian folk tales mention cats who looked like today's Norwegian Forest Cats. For a long time people believed them to be a mix of lynx and cat, and they were often referred to as "Huldrekatt" suggesting a supernatural connection, or even as Troll cats. Very early on these cats earned a place by the farmer's fireside in return for their superb mousing abilities. From time to time they would be mentioned in folk tales - Norse tales mention huge cats with lynx-like ear-tufts, and the goddess Freya's carriage was said to be drawn by a pair of white male cats from the forest.

Freya was the blond goddess of love, beauty and fecundity. Freya's Day was Friday, a popular day for marrying. It was said that if the sun shone on a wedding day, the bride had fed the cat well, meaning that she had earned the approval of the goddess's pet cats. Another story was that if farmers placed pans of milk in their cornfields for Freya's cats, the crops would flourish. Later on in history, cats which were probably Wegies were still appearing in literature such as the stories collected by Asbjørnsen and Moe in the nineteenth century. In 1912 a children's story was published by the author Gabriel Scott, all about a Norwegian Forest Cat called Sølvfaks (which translates as "silver mane").

Thus these cats were well established in the national consciousness, and Norwegians were used to having them around as an intrinsic part of their lives, but as communications improved within the country, people began to bring home cats of other breeds too. Suddenly there

©M Douglas (Vieuxtemps) "What adventure shall I dream up next?"

was a danger that these would interbreed and the native cats would become diluted. Although, as discussed in the early history section above, such varied foreign cats had been introduced long ago by the Vikings, in the twentieth century improved insulation and heating meant that cats from southern climes could easily survive for the first time in Norwegian history. Natural selection of the biggest, strongest, longest-coated cats would no longer apply. In addition, the building of roads and encroachment of towns on the wilderness began to threaten the national cat of Norway. These cats who had survived the harshest conditions over so many centuries were at risk of succumbing to the dangers brought on by modern life. So in the thirties, Norwegian cat-lovers began to think about formally recognising the Norwegian Forest Cat as a pedigree breed for the sake of its protection and, indeed, survival. The first time the breed was shown in an exhibition was 1938. But plans to protect the national cat of Norway were temporarily thwarted by the advent of the Second World War, and were not resurrected until 1963 when the Norwegian National Association of Pedigree Cats was founded. The president of this Association, Carl-Fredrik Nordane, determined that the Norwegian Forest Cat would be formally recognised for its own survival. Members of the Breeding Council set out to find good examples of their national cat, and when visiting the Oslo home of Else and Egil Nylund they found what they were looking for. Truls was such a typical specimen that they chose him as the prototype for the future of the breed. The breed was given the international name of Norwegian Forest Cat in 1972.

A dedicated group of breeders enthusiastically set about breeding Norwegian Forest Cats in a more formal way, rather than just allowing chance matings out in the wild. This was the only possible method of encouraging pure-bred Norwegian Forest Cats whose pedigrees could thenceforth be officially recorded. The Norwegian Forest Cat Circle (Norsk Skogkattring) was founded in 1975 and the Norwegian Forest Cat was provisionally recognised in 1976. The next step was to get the cat accepted by FIFe - the worldwide governing body of the cat fancy, Federation International Feline. Carl-Fredrik Nordane and Arvid Engh went to Paris to the FIFe general assembly to put forward the case for formal recognition of the Norwegian Forest Cat. They were not able to actually take cats with them, for Norway and Sweden had strict quarantine regulations, but they took photographs of Truls and other fine examples of the Norwegian Forest Cat, and persuaded the assembly to officially recognise the breed. Mrs Nordane immediately sent a wire to Norway with the good news, and Truls was the main, joyful story on Norwegian Television that evening and in Norwegian

©A Moss: Eur. Ch. Fafangens Julietta –
A beautiful Swedish female NFC behind a number of breeding cats in the UK.

newspapers the next day. This is how important the Forest Cat was to the Norwegian people. Thus the breed gained international championship status in 1977.

Because Norwegian Forest Cats had not until that time been officially "pedigree" cats, the very first pedigrees were founded on the offspring of "Novice" cats. These Novices were first-generation Forest Cats garnered from farms, villages and towns all over Norway and Sweden. Owners would present such cats to a panel of judges who would compare them to the standard set by Truls and other ideal NFCs, and if they conformed closely enough to this standard, they would be registered as first generation Norwegian Forest Cats. Three different judges were required to agree to give these cats provisional registration as NFCs. These Novices were then bred with for more than three generations, and if at any time any short-haired kittens or non-typical cats appeared, those lines were no longer used for breeding. There are lovely stories about how some of the first Norwegian Forest Cats got their names - for example Timotei, who was rescued in a very grimy state from under a car in Oslo, and given a thorough bath in a certain brand of shampoo. Novices were also collected from other FIFe countries for a time, but always the offspring of these Novices was watched carefully, and if they bred true to type from generation to generation they were deemed to be authentic pedigree Norwegian Forest Cats and were used in the breeding programme. It is quite possible that some of these Novice cats were related to other breeds, as there are a number of semi-long-haired cats both pedigree and non pedigree who may have contributed to the early NFC gene pool. However, this does not much matter as even the Norwegian Forest Cats of old would have had contributory bloodlines from the foreign cats brought in by the Vikings all those centuries ago. It is probably this very melting-pot which has given rise to the exceptional hybrid vigour exhibited throughout the breed.

Really, NFCs started off as Scandinavian "moggies" and only became pedigree cats for their own preservation. They are certainly not fancy "boudoir" cats bred to look pretty in settings devised by men, but rather exist in spite of, not because of, humankind. The important thing is that even today and beyond a Norwegian Forest Cat should look like a Forest Cat, behave like a Forest Cat, and be equipped to survive in its native country by means of size, coat quality and intelligence. There are still "real" albeit unregistered Forest Cats living on farms, or waiting on quaysides for the return of fishermen, throughout Norway - just as cats do the world over.

Thus although this is a very ancient breed, actual recording

©C&L Griffin
When they get the chance NFCs are extremely capable hunters, as shown by this young male who has been known to bring down enormous seagulls.

of individual NFCs within the registries of the cat fancy is comparatively recent. Many NFCs still exist who have pedigrees that go back only a few generations before you come across, for instance, a great-grandmother with no prefix, and just a pet name such as "Pussi". This means that that forebear was a cat straight from the farms and forests of Scandinavia, with unknown heritage behind it, but which had been proven to breed true to type. In the UK a Norwegian Forest Cat must have four generations of official pedigree history before it is allowed to be shown with the Governing Council of the Cat Fancy; however, cats from abroad with fewer generations behind them can be used for breeding so long as they are certified as being true Forest Cats. Obviously, the more years that go by, the greater the number of generations of pedigree will build up behind our cats, and because most pedigree forms show just four or five generations, soon those special "Novice" cats will cease to appear on the paperwork. No outcrossing to other breeds is permissible, but there is no need for any as the breed has such a wide gene pool.

Since that important decade of the 1970s in the history of the Norwegian Forest Cat, the Norwegian Standard has been adopted by other countries including Britain, where the Governing Council of the Cat Fancy's official description of the cat is almost identical to that of Norway/FIFe. The important features are type and coat quality, while colour is unimportant. ("Type" means the shape of the body and head.) In fact Norwegian Forest Cats come in almost every colour and pattern other than those associated with southern climates: Siamese-type pointed pattern, chocolate, lilac, cinnamon and fawn, all of which are not allowed. Some breeders in Sweden have been developing chocolate and lilac coloured NFCs, but they have not received official approval.

This desire to develop new colours affects many breeds. It is almost as though every breed will one day come in a choice of every possible colour. Maybe this is a reflection of the designer-led, consumerist society in which most of us live nowadays. There are arguments for and against these new colours:

- FOR - the colours exist anyway, so should be recognised and recorded rather than just appearing as, for instance, "brown tabby" on pedigree forms. When NFCs are walking on the wild side in their native woods, looking for a mate, they do not care what colour their coats are. Historically, cats were brought to Scandinavia from southern and eastern countries where chocolate, lilac etc. cats might already be living.

- AGAINST - Chocolate, lilac and so on would not look "natural" on a Forest Cat. It is suspected that breeders have been experimentally mixing different breeds, so the new colours are not pure-bred NFCs. Endorsement of these "artificial" colours will lead to the eventual acceptance of Siamese-pointed Norwegian Forest Cats, which I think most people would agree just wouldn't look right at all.

A possible remedy to this situation would be for breeders interested in these new colours to register them under a new breed name altogether, so that they are not mixed up with original-coloured Forest Cats. At any rate, it is important that pedigrees should clearly state what is in the background of NFCs sold for breeding so that people are aware of which lines to avoid. However, these new colours and patterns have been rejected so far and may never be officially allowed by the governing bodies of the cat fancy world-wide.

All of the following tabby patterns are seen on Norwegian Forest Cats:

"classic"	(swirls of pattern on the side of the cat with stripes elsewhere)
"mackerel"	(the very stripey pattern so often seen on many breeds)
"spotted"	(really mackerel tabby, with the stripes broken into spots)
"ticked"	(where the face has typical tabby "eye make-up" but the body is covered in evenly banded hairs giving the effect of no pattern at all, rather like a wild hare or rabbit).

©A Robinson
Ch. Magnus Möre og Romsdal, the first ticked tabby to be imported to the UK.

It is only this century that travelling became easy within most of Norway, so local areas tended to have their own predominant colour of cat. There is a small island where most cats are silver tabby, while in several areas older men and women can remember pure white Forest Cats magically appearing amongst the snow-covered trees. A resident of the Sunnmøre region (Av Borgund) relates "History speaks of natural wild packs of forest cats that have roamed the area in earlier times - packs of completely white Forest

Cats." There are brown tabbies who blend beautifully with the natural flora, and blues whose granite-coloured fur matches the rocks that are found almost everywhere. Reds, torties, creams, black and whites and smokes are also frequently seen - in fact black and white Wegies are particularly popular in Norway and Sweden.

©A Robinson (Layzell/Jarrahkatt)
Black & White is one of the most traditional and popular colours in Scandinavia, especially if the markings are symmetrical as in this fine young male neuter.

When the world pedigree cat championships were held in Munich in 1991, this ancient breed which was nonetheless a comparative newcomer to the world of pedigree cats was the top winner! World Champion Flatlands Bjørnestierne is a magnificent brown tabby bred by Rigmor Syverstad in Norway and now living in Denmark with one of the foremost breeders and geneticists, Jette Eve Madsen. Bjørnestierne means "bear star" and he is indeed a star of bear-like qualities! Since then, most World Shows have featured magnificent Norwegian Forest Cats in the finals, and there is a growing interest in the breed throughout the world. Thanks to the efforts of those first enthusiastic Norwegian breeders, the Norwegian Forest Cat will now never die out. However, all breeders must realise that they are the guardians of the Cat of the Vikings, here to preserve their natural type and character, which must not be altered in any way.

©L&G Grant (Vanaheim)
Large blue female Norwegian Forest Cat typical of those produced by world famous Danish breeder Jette Eva Madsen.

Occasionally the Scandinavian governing body approves slight refinements to the standard, but this is just to clarify certain points so that the cats' appearance does not become distorted by over-zealous breeders' exaggerating the type. For instance, in 1999 one of the proposed minor alterations to the FIFe standard is that while the ears must not be too far apart, they must also not be too close together. This is to safeguard against the undesirable exaggeration seen in some other breeds - for instance, where the nose of the Persian has become shorter and shorter until they are said to have breathing difficulties, while the head length of the Siamese has done exactly the opposite with equally extreme effects. Another change agreed in 1999 is that the coat must not be too silky. Again this is just a clarification to remind breeders and judges that above all this is, and must remain, a natural cat, with a physique rugged enough to return to the wild if need be.

However, it is undesirable that changes to the standard should be made just to fit certain powerful breeders' own cats. For instance, if a breeder were producing excellent cats whose only fault was to have weak chins, then that breeder might seek to remove the point about the chin being firm. Fortunately the Norwegian Forest Cat has guardians all over the world who would not allow such detrimental changes to take effect.

PERSONALITY

Why have Norwegian Forest Cats gained such widespread popularity? Those of us who have lived with a Wegie are in no doubt as to the reason. They

©R Jonker
This 3 month old male kitten already demonstrates the desired triangular head shape.

are not only robust and healthy, but make wonderful companions for the young and the old alike. They accept dogs, babies and other cats with calm friendship. They need very little grooming. Although they are competent to survive out of doors, their naturally relaxed outlook on life enables them to settle easily to life even in a small flat, so long as they have somewhere to jump and scratch, and plenty of company. It is often said that cats are loners, but this is not true of Norwegian Forest Cats, who love to live in a family and pine if left alone for too long. However, their companion does not have to be another Forest Cat, as they get on well with all breeds of cat as well as other animals and, of course, humans. Having a Norwegian Forest Cat at home is like living alongside a touch of wild nature, while at the same time benefiting from a very civilised and intelligent companion.

A frequently asked question is "What is the difference between the Norwegian Forest Cat and the Maine Coon?" When people are visiting a cat show, or thinking of buying a kitten, they very often get attracted to both these natural semi-longhaired breeds, but cannot really tell them apart. As a result, breeders are often requested to explain the differences. Of course, at some point there was quite possibly an intermingling of blood between the two breeds – it is probable that the Vikings had some Forest Cat-type felines on board when they landed on the east coast of America, for instance. But over the many intervening centuries distinct differences in appearance and personality have become apparent.

When studying the standards of points, and when observing good examples of each breed, it is easy enough to tell them apart visually. Both should be large, with long tails and flowing yet strong and weatherproof coats, but Forest Cats must be elegant, with long straight profiles and high set ears, together with hind legs longer than the front ones. The squarer, chunkier Maine Coons on the other hand should have a distinct curve in profile with squared off muzzle, and their ears are set wider apart. Moreover, their backs are straight and rectangular, not higher at the rear. Above all, it is the "look" of the cats which makes it obvious to which bred they belong – in the case of the Norwegian, this famous expression is engendered by the triangular face and obliquely-set eyes which look calmly down the long, straight profile. Unfortunately, you sometimes see bad examples of either breed which overlap the standards to the point where physical distinctions become lost in mediocrity.

©F Matthews
Always sociable, Wegies should not have to live alone, but are very happy to cuddle up to those they know and love.

One thing it is not so easy to detect is the difference in character between NFCs and Maine Coons, and to the pet owner, character is often the deciding factor when choosing a breed with which to share their lives. As with all breeds, there will be a great deal of variety between individuals, but nonetheless generalisations can be made.

There are some points on which most people seem to agree:

- Wegies are vocally quieter, Coonies are more talkative in a pleasant "chirruppy" kind of way. Some Wegies chirrup too, but they rarely whinge and sometimes you hardly know what their miaow sounds like.
- At the same time, Wegies are active, agile and inquisitive, while Coonies are more of a "sitting around contentedly" type of cat. Different people suit different types of cat. Wegies are certainly more demanding - some would say "naughtier" - and get bored if left alone, but they are very responsive.
- Both Wegies and Coonies are remarkably easy-going.
- Maine Coons are more easily contained, while Norwegian Forest Cats are notorious escape artists. Maine Coon owners frequently allow their cats to roam in a garden which is surrounded by a six foot high fence. This is enough to keep them safe within the grounds. I cannot imagine any NFC in a similar garden resisting scaling the fence effortlessly and immediately streaking off into the distance as they have incredible climbing abilities and an incorrigible sense of curiosity.

Wegies are notorious escapees. If you keep yours safe in an enclosed cat garden, make sure there are no weak spots on the perimeter or your Forest Cat is bound to discover them...

- Both breeds have a lot of similarities being gentle, loving cats who seem to be happy to live indoors. Wegies perhaps tend to “belong” to one special person above all others, and are more demonstrative in their affection giving passionate head-butts and face-licks.

As well as the Norwegian Forest Cat, there is another natural but lesser-known breed called the Siberian Forest Cat. Obviously cats do not recognise political boundaries, so a number of similar cats may have spread across not only Scandinavia but also Finland and the USSR in ages past. However, the standard for the two breeds varies considerably, especially when it comes to the shape of the head. Gone is the characteristic long, straight profile that makes the Wegie so unmistakable. Instead, Siberian cats have a distinct nose-break with a short, very wide head and quite different "look". Some Norwegian Forest Cats registered in Finland also have a shorter, wider head-shape than their Norwegian and Swedish cousins.

CARE

Norwegian Forest Cats are often described as "easy care" cats and this is largely true. They tend to enjoy rude good health, and take life as it comes in a sensible, un-neurotic way. This does not mean that they should be neglected however. The more time and care you give to your Forest Cat, the more it will repay you with affection, companionship and glowing good looks. NFCs are not fussy eaters and usually have robust digestions. However, they do eat quite a lot, as befits their size. It is a good idea to feed active adults with high quality dried food left down for them to eat when they want to. This can be obtained from your veterinary surgeon and will not only guard against urinary problems (brought on by too high a magnesium level in some supermarket foods) but will also help keep their teeth clean. Fresh water should always be available of course, and additional canned or fresh meat can be fed morning and/or evening. It is not necessary to provide milk. Provision of occasional oily fish such as canned sardines will keep your Forest Cat's coat in good condition. Remember, however, that vegetable oil is not digestible, so be careful to drain canned fish. Some breeders have been known to feed NFCs a diet of day-old chicks, but this is unwise. Although chicks may seem superficially similar to the small birds that would be the natural prey of Forest Cats in the wild, in reality they consist of far too much fat in relation to protein. On the other hand, proprietary canned foods contain all the vitamins and minerals needed to ensure that your cat leads a long and healthy life. Cheap cans of cat food are actually a false economy, as they simply contain more water, so you need to feed more of them. Canned and dry foods recommended by your vet are more likely to be good value in the long run, and will also assist healthy, odour-free stool formation.

The Norwegian Forest Cat, though large, should have a hard and muscular body. However, some Forest Cats - especially middle-aged neuters - do have a tendency to put on weight. This is often disguised under their luxuriant coats, but an over-round tummy can be spied at bath-time. It is easy for the loving owner to enjoy giving their beautiful, gentle cat food treats. However, if the cat shows any tendency to overweight, it is much kinder to introduce a "light" diet carefully measured according to your vet's instructions. Replace the food treats with games of "chase and fetch the silver foil ball" or "jump after the feather on a string" which your cat will appreciate even more. Norwegian Forest Cats remain playful right up to old age - so long as you keep them in practice.

Forest Cats are well known for their sense of fun.

Breeders are often asked how long a Wegie can be expected to live. This question stems from the fact that they are very large cats, and large breeds of dog are well known to have a shorter life-span than smaller breeds, so people naturally wonder if it is the same for cats. However, the difference in size between the very largest and smallest breed of cat is much less than the difference between, say, a Yorkshire Terrier and a Great Dane. Likewise, the variation in life-span is minimal between different types of cat. Norwegian Forest Cats can be expected to live for about twelve to fifteen years of age on average, although individuals may have much greater or shorter lifespans and this is just a guide. Breeders do feel that NFCs are not generally as long-lived as certain other breeds, such as oriental cats, however.

Some breeders have discovered that regular drops of Evening Primrose Oil administered along with food really improves the condition of the coat, while vets say that this wonderful oil actually helps prevent cancer too. Although it is expensive it is a worthwhile investment for your cat's looks and well-being.

It is a good idea to groom any cat once a week. Even short-haired cats benefit from this hebdomadal session, as it is an ideal time to generally check over the cat's physical condition and take note of any lumps or wounds which might otherwise remain undiscovered. Norwegian Forest Cats' coats need a long-toothed comb, which should be stroked gently through their fur right to the roots, removing any dead hairs. Some owners also use special rubber brush-combs, which the cats seem to enjoy as the result is almost like a massage. During the springtime moult, these grooming sessions should be increased to nearly every day (according to the size of your cat's coat) so that you gradually remove the woolly undercoat. This not only saves your carpet, but will also prevent the cat from swallowing too much fur, which can occasionally result in vomited fur-balls. In severe cases fur-balls can cause an internal blockage and require veterinary treatment, but generally any fur ingested seems to find its way out of one end of the cat or the other without any problem - often it can be seen in the generously-proportioned faeces. In nature, the continual scraping past twigs and bushes helps to remove unwanted undercoat, and if you have a cat-garden you will find handfuls of wool-like lumps attached to every rough surface or just blowing about in the spring breeze. It doubtless makes an excellent building material for birds' nests, going some small way to make amends for the inevitable depredation on the local bird-life which would result if your Forest Cat is allowed to roam free.

THE INDOOR/OUTDOOR DEBATE

As for being allowed out, although Norwegian Forest Cats are intelligent and sensible, they are also rather bold and inquisitive, so it is wise not to let them out without supervision. However, if trained from a young age, they love to walk on lead and harness, and they are quite content with an indoor climbing-frame, or a race up and down the stairs. It is also a good idea to build a simple, inexpensive run attached to your house so that they can get some fresh air and feel nature's breeze ripple through their coats. They really appreciate being able to lie on a high shelf and watch the world go by, or the leaves flutter in the trees. Remember, however, that they are brilliant at climbing and escaping, so be careful for their sake and yours. Any NFC who has not known total freedom will not miss it - they are so easily contented.

Should you keep your Norwegian Forest Cat indoors all its life, or allow it to roam freely? When I was owned by my first cat, a pet Siamese neuter, I wouldn't have dreamed of

©A Robinson
This pretty tortie tabby female is wearing her summer coat but still has the hint of a ruff. 2 month old daughter is wearing soft baby fur.

©E&B Hancock - (Kyrrekatt) Champagne Charli as a kitten

©R Jonker (Möre og Romsdal Kittens)

©R Jonker
(Möre og Romsdal)

©J Santillo
(Vieuxtemps St. George)

keeping her indoors. We lived literally next door to Epping Forest, a happy hunting ground throughout the year. No harm ever came from out of doors to that first cat, except for the odd flea which was easily dealt with.

As a cat breeder one has to re-think. It would be irresponsible to allow entire cats to wander freely – at the very least they would be likely to have unplanned kittens, and they are also likely to pick up diseases whilst mating with local tramp cats. I have heard some new breeders say “oh, we’ll notice when she begins to call, and keep her in then.” Doesn’t it occur to them that the ardent local tomcats will be ever so much quicker on the uptake than a mere human could ever be, and mate the fertile feline before her “owner” can grasp what is happening?

With a stud cat, of course, unwanted kittens will not be a problem – to the stud owner. But what about the unwanted babies he will foist on other females, maybe too young to give birth healthily, maybe even suffering from a disease which can be transmitted during the close contact occasioned by mating? I have heard of breeders in South Africa and Australia allowing their studs to roam free. I must say I would not want to risk the life of one of my precious boys, but if you live many miles from your nearest neighbours, it really does call for a different set of rules.

Whether to allow your cats to go outside at will is a more complicated question when it comes to neutered cats. I myself sell kittens to outside homes so long as the surroundings are suitable, and the new owners are responsible enough to keep the kitten indoors until he or she has grown old enough to be sensible. But I have heard of so many traffic deaths over the years that I am beginning to change my mind about this. Although Norwegian Forest Cats are brilliantly clever and capable in many ways, they just cannot cope with the technology that allows cars to travel faster and faster every year. You often hear people say "but my cat lived to be eighteen and went outside whenever he wanted to." But eighteen, or even ten, years ago, there were fewer cars and the world was a less crowded place! It may be that Wegies' brave and inquisitive natures make them even more vulnerable than more timid or less vivacious breeds.

Maybe the answer is to allow your cats to have access to an enclosed cat garden with plenty of room to run, snooze and play. A small but complex area is better than a large, bland one, while a wildlife pond, trees to climb and shelves on which to sunbathe will be much appreciated. To be truthful, if cats of any breed were given a choice they would prefer dangerous freedom to pampered restriction. Neutered cats who are allowed to roam have the richest and happiest life of all. Yes, they may get cold and wet. The bird population suffers. They will get torn ears and scars, which we regret and they don't care about. It is we, the humans, who worry, and miss out on sleep, and pay yet another veterinary bill. But if your cat is brought up to a safe, enclosed life from early kittenhood, he or she will never miss the freedom they have never known and you will sleep more easily in the knowledge that your beloved Wegie is safe and well. The expense of setting up a "cat garden" will soon be recouped from the savings on all those veterinary bills for abscesses and accidents that will inevitably come to cat-owners who allow their Wegie to wander. Cat gardens can be made to look as attractive as you like, with creepers growing up the sides and interior "landscaping" as elaborate as you care to make it!

©R Jonker – Exploring the cat garden for the first time...

Do be careful not to include plants that are toxic to cats however, and remember that the top should also be covered with wire if your cat is not to escape. If there is a way out, your Norwegian Forest Cat will find it! Finally, if you really do feel you live in a safe area and want your neutered pet to be allowed outside, first ensure that the breeder of your kitten is in agreement with your plans. Above all, do ensure that they are always safely at home at night - the most dangerous time of all for cats.

It is almost effortless to look after a Norwegian Forest Cat, and the hints given above could apply to almost any breed. All you really need to do are give the best diet and veterinary attention you can, a safe environment and lots of love and company. In return, your NFC will reward you a hundred-fold with affection, loud purring and surprising sensitivity to your moods. The amazingly strong bond between human and NFC is surprising to those who have not come across it before. Each individual cat has its own unique personality, and even within a litter there are huge differences in character. But every Forest Cat is loveable and rewarding, and some especially intelligent ones are almost telepathic in their understanding towards their human companions.

©J Higgins – Eur. Ch. Opatijas Big Boss – Swedish father of well-known UK stud S Charniternas Indy. (S* means Swedish import)*

NFCS IN THE UK

Because of very strict British quarantine laws, Norwegian Forest Cats reached the UK at a comparatively late date. The earliest known Forest Cat to come to the UK was imported in Bedfordshire in the late 1970s by some ladies who had lived in Norway for a while. He was a gentle giant who died at the age of seventeen, but it is not known if his parentage was recorded. All the original NFCs in the UK were, of course, imported. An Abyssinian Breeder, Alan Eagland, was visiting a big Cat Show in Amsterdam in 1986 in order to look at the Abyssinians. (The combination of Abys and NFCs is not an unusual one, even though the two breeds contrast sharply with one another. Maybe these natural, balanced breeds appeal to the same type of people.) Alan noticed some cats at the Amsterdam show with a look he had not seen before - there were at that show twenty-five large, thick-furred felines with an elegance and nobility about them that made them stand out from all the other breeds present. He made enquiries and discovered that these remarkable cats, which looked so wild but behaved so gently, were Norwegian Forest Cats - a breed previously unheard of to most of the English speaking world. Eagerly Alan began to ask questions of the breeders at that show, and after many months and several more visits to Holland he arranged for the importation of four Norwegian Forest Cats into the UK. These were the foundation stock of his Norsechat breeding line. He chose a brown tabby and white male (the colour of the original Truls), and three females: a brown tabby, who went on to produce more than fifty kittens; a black smoke; and a tortie and white. The stud's name was Torv Hede's Knurre Bjørn, which translates as "Growling Bear". Alan admits that not all of the first imports were of a very high quality, because he and everyone else in the UK were newcomers to the breed and had no ideal with which to compare the cats.

Coincidentally, while Alan England was discovering Norwegian Forest Cats a lady called Gill Hart was moving back to England from Norway, where she had been living for some years. While in Norway Gill had fallen in love with their national breed of cat and got to know a lot about what a Norwegian Forest Cat should look like. She lived in Stavanger and bred Persians and Norwegian Forest Cats under the prefix Høvedmanngärd, including a number of titled cats. When the time came for Gill to return to her native England, she reluctantly decided she had to rehome all her cats in Norway as she could not bear the thought of them undergoing the necessary long quarantine. However, once in Britain, she missed her Norwegian Forest Cats and decided to start breeding again under a new prefix - Trahkatt, which comes from her surname spelt backwards. Gill set about trying to get recognition for the NFC with the GCCF, and translated the Norwegian standard of points. The GCCF would not readily accept some of the phrases used in the standard - which is why ours differs slightly from the FIFe standard even today. For instance, the GCCF did not like the use of the word "triangular" which describes the shape of the Wegie face. There was a lot of to-ing and fro-ing between Gill, the GCCF and Norway, until eventually the standard was acceptable and put in place in the UK. At the same time, Gill joined Alan in setting up the Norwegian Forest Cat Club. She edited the Club's Newsletter and did a lot of research on the new generation of Forest Cats being imported into the UK. She was determined that we should get the right cats over here - big cats with correct coat quality and, above all, with long, straight profiles. It is small, round heads with less than straight profiles which spoil the look of many substandard Norwegian Forest Cats. Gill's advice to this day is: "Always look for the most extreme kitten in a litter."

©R Jonker
Promising 6 month old tortie tabby and white female with typical NFC expression.

Gill Hart and Alan Eagland worked hard starting up the Norwegian Forest Cat Club, which was formed in the UK in 1987. Soon other breeders began to fall in love with these wonderful animals but although Gill is a still a life member of the Club, by a desperate stroke of bad luck she became ill and had to give up her NFC breeding programme. Unfortunately Gill suffered from asthma, and was dangerously affected by living in close proximity to her beautiful Norwegian Forest Cats. As a result of hospitalisation, she had to give up breeding and her cats were taken over by other early British breeders. Her magnificent black and white stud, King Vincent av Huldrepus, continued to sire quality kittens for several years for the Tarrakatt cattery on England's south coast, while further studs and queens were imported by other breeders. Indeed, a number of Forest Cats are still brought in almost every year from Norway, Sweden, Holland and Denmark right up to this day. As a result, although we live in a small island, we have a good variety of bloodlines in Britain which is all for the strengthening of the breed over here. Gradually breeders have learned more and more, and many have made their way to Norway and Sweden where they have seen magnificent specimens at shows and in people's homes.

Although these special cats might well not have been officially introduced to Britain had it not been for Gill Hart and Alan Eagland, the way to get a breed noticed is to take the cats to GCCF shows, and now it was the turn of Alan Watt to get involved. Having taken advice from Gill, he imported his first two cats - tortie silver tabby and white female Gaupeskogens Gerry Hall and blue tabby and white male Asvangens Ulfrun - but not without difficulty. They ended up catching flu while in quarantine, and Alan and Sheila had to deal with eye ulcers upon their release. Undeterred, they became familiar figures at cat shows with their Skogens prefix, displaying and talking about their favourite breed, and arranging the first Norwegian Forest Cat seminar in 1990 so as to educate judges and all those who were becoming interested in the breed. Alan also worked at setting up a Committee and Constitution for the Norwegian Forest Cat Club, with the first secretary being Gill Hart, followed by Sue Saville who bred under the Dilettante prefix.

©R&D Dobson (Maysula) – NFC kittens are extremely inquisitive and ready to try anything to satisfy their huge appetites.

All the importing was extremely costly, but right from the start Alan Watt felt that the price of kittens should not be made out of reach of ordinary people, and the usual price charged was around £250. (At the time of writing kittens now cost from £250-£350, which is still good value considering that so many cats continue to be imported.)

During 1990 a total of twenty-one NFCs competed and won merits at shows in Britain. The prefixes which appeared on the showbench in that year were Skogens, Dilettante, Mousebane (Hannah Money's prefix), Tarrakatt and Eddan (Swedish import). These then were the people and cats who paved the way for those of us who fell in love with the breed in the following years.

When importing a cat, especially from Norway, it is always difficult to procure a prime specimen as there is a variety of good and bad over there just as there is everywhere. Many Norwegian breeders may have preferred not to export to a country which had such harsh quarantine regulations; until recently, all Norwegian Forest Cats had to suffer six months incarcerated in a quarantine cattery even if they came from rabies-free countries such as Norway and Sweden. Nowadays the Balai Directive, and "Passports for Pets" initiative, mean that it is much easier for Norwegian Forest Cats to cross the North Sea. But fortunately good cats were allowed to come over from Scandinavia and Northern Europe from time to time, and as the English and Scottish breeders became more experienced they managed to obtain excellent breeding stock. In 1995 it was estimated that there were approximately 1,000 NFCs in the UK while by the end of 1998 there were nearly 1500. As a result, the breed has gone from strength to strength as we have learned to judge just what a true Norwegian Forest Cat should look like. Some experienced British breeders have even had the honour of stewarding and judging at cat shows in Scandinavia, and nowadays cats are often exported from, as well as into, the UK.

In Europe catteries often have suffixes instead of prefixes, such as Jette Eva Madsen's famous suffix Felis Jubatus, which translates as "cat with a mane".

Many show winners abroad and in the UK can trace their ancestry to Felis Jubatus lines. Another well-known prefix here and abroad is Frostnattens, while some of the first cats in the UK carried the names Av Huldrepus, Torv Hede's, Charniternas, Eddan, Gaupeskogens, Norodden and Tronderskogens.

©P&A Bowler (Skjonn)
Four month old kitten – litter sister of the first female premier in the UK.

In 1997, ten years after the foundation of the Norwegian Forest Cat Club, the Governing Council of the Cat Fancy in Britain awarded Championship Status to the Norwegian Forest Cat. This meant that enough kittens were being bred from a sufficiently wide breeder base and that a number of quality cats were gaining awards on the showbench. Championship Status only came after Wegies had been on the British show scene for a number of years. The first NFCs to be imported into Britain had been given "experimental" status by the Governing Council of the Cat Fancy. Although they were an ancient breed, and no-one was doing any experimenting with them, this status reflected the fact that

©A Robinson
This green eyed white male was the very first NFC to gain a title in the UK. Premier Vieuxtemps Impromptu owns and was proudly bred by the author.

they were very new to the UK. Moreover, they were put in the "Foreign Shorthair" section at first, until the much more appropriate "Semi Long Hair" section was set up. They could compete with other breeds in side classes at GCCF shows and also have their own open classes. If the judges considered that the NFCs competing in the Open were of sufficient quality, they would be awarded a Merit Certificate. At this stage, Forest Cats were not in competition with each other in the Open. They were each compared with the breed standard of points (which had to be displayed on the top of each cat's pen) and if all the cats in the Open class matched that standard, then all would be given a Merit Certificate. Fortunately a considerable number of Norwegian Forest Cats of distinction appeared on the showbench at this time and won enough merits for the breed to progress to Intermediate Status in 1995. The GCCF requirement from this point was that at least twenty Norwegian Forest Cats must win three Intermediate Certificates each in their open classes, in which they were now also competing against each other. Only one certificate was awarded for each open class from now on, so it was getting more difficult. But within two years enough cats had won enough certificates for the breed to go on to gain Championship Status in June 1997 (June is the beginning of the GCCF Show Year.) From now on there would be titled Norwegian Forest Cats in Britain, just as there had been in Europe for many years.

The very first Norwegian Forest Cat to gain a title in Britain was Premier Vieuxtemps Impromptu, a green-eyed white boy whose nature was as generous as his coat and size. Following this, many beautiful Norwegian Forest Cats gained the titles of Champion, Premier, and even Grand Champion and Grand Premier. The first "Grand" NFC in the UK was a large silver tabby and white female neuter, Grand Premier Maysula Helenya, who also effortlessly won the very first UK Grand Certificate at the Supreme Show in 1998.

Owners and breeders were proud to see their Wegies winning in competition against other, more established, breeds, and special mention has to be made of two stunning Norwegian Forest Cats who won the accolade of Best In Show in large all-breed shows not once, but over and over again. Cats often number in many hundreds at British shows, so this is no mean feat.

©C&L Layzell (Jarrahkatt)
The UK's first grand titled cat – Grand Premier Maysula Helenya, bred by Roger and Doreen Dobson and owned/shown/adored by Shirley and Ivan Lazell. Here she is relaxing at home.

©E&B Hancock
Grand Champion Kyrrekatt Claire, owned/bred by Eileen and Brian Hancock.

Grand Champion Kyrrekatt Claire, the first Grand Champion Norwegian Forest Cat in the UK, was Overall Best in Show four times well before she was even two years old. She is another solid white Forest Cat - a true "Snowcat" - with unbelievably bright blue eyes. Claire gets her name from her great-grandmother, a famous blue-eyed white cat who literally walked out of a forest near Oslo and joined a family in whose home she had a single litter before she was tragically killed in a car accident. Her progeny live on, however, and number many titled show winners throughout Europe. No doubt the second Claire will contribute to the continual improvement in type the UK breeders seek. At the time of writing, Claire has attained Best in Show no fewer than nine times!

Another great ambassador for the breed, silver tabby Grand Premier Lizzara Bardolph - or Wolfie as he is known at home - has attained Overall Best in Show on three separate occasions, and has won countless first prizes. He was born in Surrey in July 1993, and his huge size always draws many onlookers to his double-width show pen, while his eyes are as bright a green as Claire's are blue. "Bardolph" means "Bright Wolf" but although he does indeed shine on the showbench, this veteran prefers to relax at home with a little snack or four.

CHOOSING AN NFC KITTEN

Maybe reading all about how very special Wegies are makes you wish that you, too, had one of these irresistible feline companions at home! If you are thinking along those lines, first you have to decide why you want an NFC kitten. Is it to be a family pet, or maybe you would like to show your kitten? If you are interested in becoming a breeder, you may find the section on breeding of help.

©M Douglas (Vieuxtemps) A kitten aged 9 weeks.

©K&J Digweed The same kitten aged 4 months – still an innocent expression.

If you are just choosing a family pet, all that matters is that you choose a kitten that appeals to you, and is healthy, of good character and well-brought-up. If you would like a show neuter, you have to be a little more careful, as your kitten needs to conform closely to the Standard of Points if you are to have any success. It is wise to go to a few shows and see which cats you like the look of, and which prefixes do most of the winning, before you make your final choice. (A "prefix" is the special name that appears at the beginning of a cat's pedigree name, and indicates which breeder the cat comes from.) In any case you should never buy a single kitten if you have no other friendly pets, and go out to work all day. The intelligence

©K&J Digweed The same kitten at 6 months – Definitely a more "knowing" look!

©C Henderson
Norwegian Forest Cats love living with other breeds of cat. Here a full-grown male neuter is typically helping his Bengal friend to look after her kittens.

and gregariousness of the NFC would mean that it was lonely and unhappy, even though it would make the best it could of its surroundings. Norwegian Forest Cats deserve better than that, so if you cannot afford to buy two kittens from the same litter, you should arrange for a second kitten or young cat to join you at the same time, maybe from a rescue centre. NFCs are not racist and make friends with moggies as well as other breeds!

Of course, if you have the most typical, beautiful NFC in the world, yet it is bad-tempered or unhealthy, then it will be a great disappointment to you and may even adversely affect the other members of your household. Fortunately, most NFCs have interesting and adorable characters, but there are exceptions. Character is heavily influenced by genetics – the nature of a kitten's father is especially important. The way that the kitten has been brought up is also vital – has it had plenty of handling in the crucial first few weeks of its life? Is it used to meeting a variety of people and maybe other animals too? Has it been brought up indoors as part of the family, so that it is used to normal household noises and activities?

©K&J Digweed
Even when relaxing, NFC kittens are alert and ready to play at the least invitation.

Health is also absolutely essential, and the least you can expect when you have taken the trouble to carefully select a pedigree breed is a robust, fully wormed and inoculated kitten who has been given the best possible diet and physical care.

How do you avoid cats that are of poor character or delicate in health? Fortunately it is easy to spot a bad tempered cat! Most kittens are sweet in their behaviour, although some may be timid. But study the character of the mother and, if possible, the father. Their response to you as a stranger will indicate what they are like. When choosing a kitten, spend as much time as possible watching the whole litter and especially, the parents.

Good health is also to a certain extent apparent. When choosing a kitten, ensure that it is a good size for its age (i.e. at least 1lb/0.5kg per month). Does it have bright eyes, clean ears, glossy coat and a clean bottom? Is it alert and interested in everything that is going on around it? If in doubt, try to get an experienced breeder to accompany you on your visit when you go to choose a kitten. They will be used to what a kitten should be like at each stage of life. **Never, never buy a kitten just because you feel sorry for it!**

Warning: Norwegian Forest Cats are addictive! You may, like me, end up with more than one - or three - or nine...

BREEDING FOREST CATS

Generally speaking, NFCs are a good choice for both novice breeders and those who have started with another breed but are looking for involvement in a second. NFCs are natural cats and do not have many inherent defects. There is a very wide gene pool available, even in the UK, and temperamentally they could hardly be easier to live with. Many people who are used to other, more volatile, breeds of cat are surprised and delighted when they discover just how loveable and easy-going NFCs are to live with. I started off with Siamese and Orientals, and to this day I am amazed at how quiet and undemanding is the voice of my Wegies. Moreover, NFCs come in a wide choice of colours and it is possible to end up with a variety of kittens in each litter if you want – which not only looks very charming but also makes them attractive to potential purchasers. Alternatively, you may decide you prefer one particular coat colour and concentrate on that. In any case colour is not considered important in the breed, as it is type, coat quality and character for which NFCs are famous. There are none of those problems of getting exactly the right markings as there are in, for instance, Birmans and Abyssinians. Because breeders have had little incentive to "improve" the colour of their NFCs, black coats can often appear rusty-brown, while silver tabbies frequently suffer from "tarnishing" which is a yellowing of what should really be true monochrome tones. Brown tabbies, which in other breeds are usually rich in tone, can be quite dull in Norwegian Forest Cats. This should not be counted against the cats when being judged at a show, although if there were two cats of virtually equal merit, then the judge would be likely to award the top position to the cat with the most true coat colour. Because colour and pattern are not important it is type, size and coat quality which it is vital we should "get right". However, if you feel you would like to concentrate on obtaining excellent colour as well as excellent type in your breeding programme, there is nothing wrong with that, so long as you ensure that considerations of type always comes first.

What do we mean by "type"? Every breeder – novice or experienced – should constantly remind themselves of the breed Standard of Points. This is very similar for both the GCCF in the UK and FIFe, the main governing body throughout Scandinavia and Europe. If we are breeding NFCs, then they should look like NFCs and not like moggies, Maine Coons or any other breed! A good NFC should be immediately identifiable as such – they should have that unmistakable "NFC look". Of course nobody breeds kittens who are one hundred percent perfect, but nonetheless every kitten should be recognisable as clearly belonging to its breed. Because there are comparatively few NFCs being bred in the UK to date, every single breeding cat has an influence on the way the breed will look in future. This is a big responsibility for breeders! So each breeder must ensure that they breed true to type, according to the Standard of Points, rather than just breeding in a manner which is merely convenient or chance-led.

How do you decide what is good or bad type? Some people find it easier than others to judge the quality of a cat. A good cat or kitten is not necessarily the prettiest one available. Sometimes the very best type NFC kittens look quite strange from 8 weeks to 8 months or older. Conversely, a poor example of an NFC can still be very attractive as a cat – it could look like an old-type Persian, or an elegant Oriental for instance – both beautiful cats in their own right but not NFCs! Even if you have a "good eye" you need to keep in practice by looking at other people's cats and above all you need to be very critical of your own cats. If you have a special favourite cat, do not let him or her cast a spell on you so that you think the cat is actually a better example of the breed than it really is.

©R Jonker – (Möre og Romsdal)
9 week old kittens already demonstrating the long straight profile demanded by the NFC standard.

©M Douglas (Vieuxtemps)
One of the same kittens as a 2 year old adult – the straight profile has not deteriorated.

Obviously, health and character are just as important as correct appearance in any breeding cat. Health is essential in a cat who is to be used for breeding – for although cats seem to take motherhood very calmly, birthing does take a lot out of them, and any weakness of constitution might well be passed on to the kittens.

How can one obtain a queen with good type? To choose a breeding cat of correct appearance is not only essential but probably the most difficult task. This is because there are certain features which are only apparent at birth which then reappear after ten weeks of age. So if you visit a kitten aged four to nine weeks, even if you know what you are looking for, it will be very difficult to tell how the kitten will develop as an adult. For instance, NFCs should have completely straight profiles.

A good kitten will be born with a straight nose, but as soon as it starts to suckle from its mother its nose will get squashed into a retroussé shape that may take weeks or even months to straighten out. Likewise, the tail – which should be long – varies from one week to the next as the kitten grows different parts of its body in spurts! So a certain amount of judgement has to be made on the basis of an educated guess. Above all, the kitten's lines (ancestors) need to be taken into consideration. How have other cats of previous, similar matings developed? (The breeder should have photos available to show you. Sometimes promising kittens turn into disappointing adults.) A common fault in some lines is that a cat's head becomes far too short as it

©R Jonker (Möre og Romsdal)
At 3 weeks NFC kittens give little impression of the large elegant cats they will become in adulthood.

reaches adulthood, even though it may have been correctly proportioned as a kitten. How do the parents look? Does their appearance match the Standard of Points? Are they a good size? If it is between the months of October and March, do they have good coats with defined ruffs, knickerbockers and shirt-fronts? (Sometimes a mother cat moults when she has her kittens in a warm indoor environment, so ask to see a photo of her in full coat if you cannot see for yourself.) You will be paying a lot of money for your new kitten (or if not, that may be suspicious) so you are entitled to ask these questions and be careful in your choice.

It is a good idea to choose a queen for her type, good boning and coat quality rather than just for preferred colour, although if you are patient (or lucky) you may get all four qualities in one cat. Work out a shortlist of your preferred breeders and visit as many as possible. It is only when you see a cat in its own home surroundings that you can see how it is looked after and what it is really like. You will probably visit your chosen kitten for the first time when she is one or two months old. If someone tries to sell you an older kitten, it is best to be cautious, as why would a really good kitten be left unsold so long? However, there may be special circumstances where a good older kitten is available – for instance, a breeder might have considered one particular kitten too good to sell as a pet, and be waiting for a show/ breeding home to come along. You will discover the other side of this coin once you are selling kittens yourself!

If a breeder says a kitten is suitable for breeding but not showing, think twice. A consistently show-winning cat is one that is a good example of the breed. A cat unsuitable for showing may well be a poor example of the breed. Why then would you breed from an inferior example? Is the breeder just trying to off-load a poor quality kitten for which they have failed to find a pet home? This is a difficult question, as there are certain circumstances where non-show queens make nonetheless good breeding queens. For example, I know a very beautiful queen whose ear got torn as a kitten. She cannot be shown, but the fault is superficial and not genetic and will not therefore affect her offspring. There is a saying "it is better to buy a poor cat from a good line than a good cat from a poor line." The underlying genetic factors are what will influence how your kittens develop. But to be on the safe side, always buy a show quality cat for breeding. And as a breeder, you should always show as much as possible – that is the only way you will be able to ensure that your cats are up to standard. Breeding by yourself at home, with no comparisons possible, may lead you to produce cats that are unintentionally damaging to the breed.

In genetics there are few certainties, and two good quality cats will not always produce excellent kittens although this is much more likely than if you mate two bad examples of the breed. Your queen may have been calling for many months by the time she is 15 months old, or perhaps she is a late developer and will only begin to come into season at one year old. Because they have such a varied background, NFCs do tend to vary in this and many other ways and you often have to "play it by ear". Sometimes this is literal, as a calling queen can be very vocal. Others are "silent callers" whose behaviour you have to watch carefully to tell when they are in season. Norwegian Forest queens tend to come on heat at a time of year to coincide with birth in good weather – i.e. lots of spring babies and not many autumn/winter ones, which is very sensible in the wild. However, with central heating, some cats do call all the year round, while others only call once or twice in twelve months.

©R Jonker (Möre og Romsdal)
Females, whilst retaining that wild look and distinctive expression, often have shorter faces and a more feminine appearance.

Timing of births varies considerably between individual queens, but an average litter of 5 kittens could take about three and a half hours from the first "breaking of the waters". Each kitten is likely to take between fifteen minutes and up to one hour to be born. Usually a queen's instincts are strong enough for her to do the right thing, and all you need to do is to watch. However, if you are at all worried, call the vet - your queen is too precious to risk her life, and even if you end up paying a hefty bill that is better than your cat suffering and maybe ending her breeding career.

Assuming at all goes well, after a few hours you will be gazing adoringly at a number of little damp, sausage-shaped bodies. Experienced breeders are often able to check the quality of the kittens at this point - do they have perfectly straight profiles before they begin to suckle? Are their tails long enough to reach to the bottom of their back legs? You may not be able to tell the colour of the kittens at this point – sometimes brown tabby and whites look like black and whites, while the red of a tortie may not show up for a few hours or even days. If your queen is blue and you think you have a blue kitten, check with the stud owner because if he doesn't carry dilute, a blue kitten would be genetically impossible.

At about ten days after the birth, a mother cat will often try to move her kittens to another spot. If possible, pre-empt this by choosing another quiet, warm, clean and safe place which is equally convenient to you as the first one. This relocation instinct relates to the fact that, in the wild, the nest would become soiled due to the birth and might begin to smell, thus attracting predators. Also, the kittens will be beginning to crawl and squeak a lot more now, so the queen would like them to be somewhere very private.

After about three to four weeks the kittens will be toddling around quite adeptly, and beginning to show an interest in eating something other than long-suffering mum. They experiment with cat litter, blankets, human fingers – anything that their sharp little teeth come across. At this point you can begin to introduce weaning foods, such as Hill's Feline Growth mixed with made-up Lactol, or a little chopped-up breast of chicken. (Do not use meat from the supermarket delicatessen counter though as this contains inappropriate chemicals.) You should leave a dish of water and a dish of high quality dry kitten food down at all times, and often the first sign of weaning is a kitten munching away of its own accord. Once one catches on, the rest will follow, but keep an eye on them to make sure they are all weaned by about five weeks, and if one or two are slow learners encourage them by giving them tit-bits by hand for a while. Many breeders "help" the weaning process by introducing human baby foods, or cereal mixed with milk, but I personally do not think this is a good idea as where would Wegies find baby food or cereal in the Scandinavian forests? As soon as kittens start to eat solid foods they also need to be taught to use the litter tray. Be gentle but firm at all times. Keep the litter tray clean, but do not scrub it out at first, as its slight smell will guide the kittens where to go. Ensure that all kittens get their share, and that food, water and a clean litter tray are available at all times throughout the day or night. It is impossible to overfeed a kitten.

If you become a really serious breeder of Norwegian Forest Cats and would like to import your own queen or stud, do be very careful because not all cats that are bred in Scandinavia are automatically wonderful examples of the breed. Just as over here, there is a complete mix of types, levels of health and breeder responsibility. It is also unwise to import a cat based solely on information gained over the Internet. However, with the relaxation of the quarantine laws you may be able to import a cat more easily than it has been for the earliest breeders of Norwegian Forest Cats. Should you get the chance to visit some cat shows in Europe you will be able to

©R Jonker (Möre og Romsdal)

see tens, maybe hundreds, of NFCs all at one show. Contrastingly, in the UK there are usually less than ten NFCs at a show, although there have been several times that number at the annual breed show of the Norwegian Forest Cat Club. If - once you are experienced enough to trust your own judgement - you do choose to import an NFC, it would be good if at least part of his or her bloodlines were completely fresh to the UK. (For instance, nearly all the cats over here have a cat called Pan's Polaris in their bloodlines so it is good to try and get different lines from these, so long as they have the "look" you want.)

Although NFCs are generally a very healthy breed, this does not mean that every kitten is born in perfect health. Generally speaking, litters are robust and hearty, but every now and then a problem crops up. One problem quite common to pure white NFCs is deafness. In fact deafness is connected to white-coated cats of most breeds. This does not mean that all, or even most, white NFCs are hard of hearing, but some are - so if you want to breed this colour you have to be especially aware of this potential problem. In an indoor environment white cats lead full and happy lives, and are often reported to be even more sweet natured and responsive than fully hearing cats.

Another quite frequent problem is that of tail faults. This fault is a genetic defect officially listed by the GCCF, and to take such cats to shows is forbidden. It is also inadvisable to breed from cats who have tail faults, or whose littermates have such faults. In reality a tail fault can be a tiny bump on the end of the tail, or two bones fused together near the end. It is often such a tiny thing that it is difficult to feel even when you try. The reason the GCCF view such faults as serious, however, is because the tail is part of the spine and if such cats are bred together eventually much more lethal deformities may appear. It is a case of "nipping problems in the bud". Apparently a condition known as "flat chestedness" is occasionally seen in NFC kittens in Europe, but this should be clearly evident after a cursory physical examination.

As NFCs have naturally shaped heads and bodies they do not suffer from the problems associated with the very short faces or emaciated elongation of some other breeds. However, as breeders we must all be careful to ensure that the proportions of our NFCs remain unaltered. Chins must not become weak. Bodies and faces must not become excessively short or long. When breeding, we must be constantly aware of the Standard of Points so that we are not guilty of changing the look of the cat in the way that some other breeds have changed over a very short time. That is why we breeders have such a responsibility in this small island of ours – protect, nourish and promote our breed wherever you can, but do so unselfishly and if we work together our reward will be to see the breed go from strength to strength during our lifetimes.

SHOWING NFCS

Every Norwegian Forest Cat that was ever born is beautiful, and generally we truly believe that our own cats are the most beautiful of all. However, if you are interested in showing, you need to take care in your choice of kitten so that it will have a reasonable chance of success on the showbench. Choose from the stock of an established breeder, and ensure when you buy your kitten that the breeder considers it to be of potential show quality. No-one can sell a guaranteed show winner, although experienced breeders and showers can make an educated guess at which kitten is "pick of litter". Never show a kitten if the breeder asks you not to, as it would not be fair to show in public a kitten which was not up to that breeder's usual standard. It is often worth waiting for a really superb kitten, because most reputable breeders are proud for their best kittens to be seen on the showbench.

©A&P Bowler (Skjonn)
One week old Wegie baby with eyes still closed and ears well down the side of the head, quite unrecognisable from the magnificent adult type.

If you have a good kitten, and your breeder agrees that it is a good idea to show, the breeder will doubtless give you a lot of helpful advice. Different coats require varied show preparation routines, but the thing to remember is to ensure that your NFC has clipped front claws, clean ears and nose and spotless fur. Any white areas should be unstained, and even darker coats may need a shampoo a few days before a show in order to get rid of any debris, dandruff or excess grease. A common problem, particularly with males, is "stud tail" which is a brownish staining at the roots of the tail fur, about half way down the tail. This is easily dealt with by a quick application of washing up liquid carefully rinsed out, or in severe cases, a dose of Swarfega (the latter to be applied to dry fur, then washed off)! It is a good idea to occasionally perform this quick and simple operation even on house pets, as the excess grease can lead to blocked pores and bacteria build-up. In any case, if you get your kitten used to being bathed when young, then if a potentially fatal accident ever occurs - such as your cat getting covered in oil paint, which it will try to lick off - you will be more easily able to clean the soiled feline. Unlike most other breeds, Norwegian Forest Cats usually enjoy bath-time and may even try to join you in your own personal ablutions! However, both cats and humans are individuals, and it is not unknown for top show-winners to have never had a bath in their lives. It is simply a case of trial and error to find out what is best for you and your cat.

A pedigree, un-neutered kitten may be shown between the ages of 14 weeks and 9 months. The moment it reaches the grand old age of 9 months it officially becomes an adult! If you are intending to keep the cat as a show neuter, you can either continue to show it “entire” for a while or, if you prefer, get it neutered and show it as a neuter as soon as it has recovered from the operation. Males usually recover within two to three weeks, while females will take several months to grow back the fur which is shaved away during the operation. In any case it is a good idea to mention to the vet that your cat is a show cat, so that fur can be shaved discreetly and as little as possible. The time it takes to grow back varies with the individual cat and also with the time of year.

It is a good idea to take your kitten to as many shows as possible, so that he or she gets entirely used to the whole day out and probably grows to love the attention. Once you have been to a few shows, you will hopefully have collected some attractive rosettes and maybe even had your cat made up to Champion or the neutered equivalent, Premier. If this happens, you can think about entering the Grand Classes, where the very best cats compete with one another for the title of Grand Premier or Grand Champion.

©Mary-Rose Douglas (Vieuxtemps)

The most important show in the GCCF calendar is the Supreme show, usually held in the National Exhibition Centre at Birmingham. This is a super show to visit, as it is run on different lines from other shows and people are allowed to decorate their pens how they like. Cats and kittens need to qualify to enter the Supreme Show. Even if you are not interested in showing, it is well worth a visit to the Supreme Show because a number of the best NFCs in Britain will undoubtedly be present.

WEGIES ACROSS THE GLOBE

Norwegian Forest Cats are known by local names abroad. In Norway it is the Skaukatt or Skogkatt, or more formally as the Norsk Skogkatt. "Skog" is Norwegian for wood(s). Its nickname both here and in Norway is "Wegie", pronounced "Weejie". In France the breed is known as "Chat des Bois Norvégien" while the Germans call it the Norwegische Waldkatze.

Norwegian Forest Cats are much loved in Finland, the first NFC being imported from Norway in 1979. By the late 1990s around 2,000 NFCs were registered, with around 200 kittens a year being added. Norwegian Forest Cats are not only enthusiastically nurtured in their native Scandinavia. They can now be found throughout Europe as well as in the United States, Australia, South Africa and Japan. Norwegian Forest Cats were introduced to the USA a few years before they reached the UK. Only sixteen were registered in 1982, but after that numbers really took off and today they are very popular, although they have developed to a slightly different standard. This may have been because the American cat fancy was keen to differentiate between NFCs and the native Maine Coon, or perhaps the American people generally prefer a different type of cat. To look at American NFCs it is easy to see that they have shorter faces, smaller and wider apart ears with rounded tops, less elongated bodies and generally lacking the typical expression of those found in Europe.

It is difficult to imagine these Nordic felines settling in Australia, but their easy-care good looks and confident characters have won the hearts of Australians as they have elsewhere. There are now steadily increasing numbers of

Forest Cats in Australia and they are already beginning to win titles at antipodean cat shows. There is also increasing interest in the breed in South Africa, where the handful of NFC breeders is being augmented each year.

NFCs were introduced to Japan slightly later than they were to the UK. The first NFC imported into Japan was Wegiekatt's Dane of Pa Dane, who was born in 1988. Most people in Japan have still not heard of the Norwegian Forest Cat, but as is the case over here, interest is increasing and the number of breeders is growing.

Now that many are on the Internet, breeders across the globe find it easier to stay in touch and learn about each others' cats by linking with other web-pages and developing e-mail friendships. The website address of the Norwegian Forest Cat Club in the UK is:

www.catbreeder.co.uk/sites/nfcc

In any small breed population the foundation imports have a huge influence at first, so far-flung lands must continually look to Scandinavia to check that their breeding is not drifting away from the original, very special look that is the Norwegian Forest Cat.

This symbol is used by many Norwegian Forest Cat Clubs throughout the world. It shows the typical "smile" made by the shape of the Forest Cat's mouth.

Acknowledgements:

Many thanks to all my friends and fellow-breeders who provided pictures and information towards this book. In particular, I have to thank Rudy Jonker who provided so many wonderful photographs.

MRD